# *The*
# PUBLISHED
# PROFESSIONAL

## HOW SELF-PUBLISHING CAN HELP BUILD YOUR BRAND, ATTRACT MORE CLIENTS, AND INCREASE SALES

**ROB ARCHANGEL**

www.ArchangelInk.com

Published by

www.archangelink.com

ISBN-10: 1-942761-85-6

ISBN-13: 978-1-942761-85-3

# CONTENTS

PREFACE - HOW ONE MAN EARNED $70,000 BY ACCIDENT     1

INTRODUCTION     5

CHAPTER 1 - 20 REASONS YOU SHOULD WRITE A BOOK     13

CHAPTER 2 - THE COST OF INACTION: REASONS NOT TO DELAY     23

CHAPTER 3 - HOW ARCHANGEL INK HELPS YOU TELL YOUR STORY     29

CHAPTER 4 - TOP 10 WAYS TO LEVERAGE YOUR BOOK     37

CHAPTER 5 - TESTIMONIALS     53

EPILOGUE     59

ABOUT THE AUTHOR     63

# CONTENTS

# PREFACE

## HOW ONE MAN EARNED
## $70,000 BY ACCIDENT

Real estate agent Alex Goldstein crafted a short e-book on seller-financing a home after the housing market crash several years ago. He distributed it on Craigslist briefly before moving on to other marketing avenues. But something odd happened.

With the book in circulation, he started receiving calls from potential clients ready to do business. They weren't numerous, but they were the *right kind* of clients. Working with them was easy; they trusted his expertise, valued his advice, worked on his terms, and rarely (if ever) haggled over price. They were highly prequalified and presold on him specifically, not just his industry, and increased his revenue while making his job easier.

In a way, he was annoyed. As Alex tells this story in his book *Publish to Sell: Long Term Income from Short Term Effort*, he describes how direct marketing and advertising required more coordination and a lot of prospect pre-qualifying. How was it that this little book—something he hadn't put effort into in years—was more effective than what he continued to spend so much time, money and energy on?

But he got over it, accepted the lesson, and enjoyed the results. When all was tallied, he'd earned $70,000 in commissions as a direct result of his first book.

# INTRODUCTION

Alex's story isn't a fluke. Every business owner in the world can reach target clients using the same tool Alex discovered. If you haven't yet considered writing a book, you're missing an opportunity to broadcast your story, build your brand, and bring your business to the next level.

With the self-publishing options available today, it's easier than ever to make your words available to tens, hundreds, thousands—even millions—of readers and potential prospects. The technical barriers are essentially gone.

With such a low bar for entry, competition is high, and royalty proceeds are often low. Most authors will never sit atop a national bestseller list. But as a business owner, you can still publish profitably even if you don't sell many copies. The secret Alex discovered is that business owners can utilize their book as a working *business card* to court clients, establish credibility, and build prestige within their industry.

It's a niche not yet widely tapped into, though that will change as time goes on. Taking action now, rather than months or years down the road when the market is more saturated, positions you far ahead of your competition.

But what if you don't have the time, interest, or skills to write a book? What if you lack the knowledge it takes to navigate all the intricacies of publishing? Consider the wisdom of Warren Buffett.

Mike Flint was the personal pilot to Warren Buffett. Discussing goals and priorities, Buffett asked him to list his Top 25 Goals, and then told him to select five to focus on.

Buffett then asked Flint what he would do about the other items, to which his pilot answered, paraphrasing: "They'll still get my attention, and I'll focus on them as I'm able to alongside my top five."

Buffett replied, "No. Going forward, you *avoid these tasks at all costs*. No matter what, don't focus on them until you've completed your other goals."[1]

Why?

They are siren songs, seductive goals and visions that hold sway over your heart and mind, but not so much sway that they are worth actually prioritizing. Instead, they will take time and energy away from that which, on reflection, is of greatest value.

To avoid this, you must be ruthless, and ruthlessly honest with yourself. In other words, eliminate and prioritize. Make effective time-management decisions.

As a business owner, you have only so much bandwidth, so use it wisely. You don't have to learn the ins and outs of the publishing world yourself to be able to reach potential clients with your story. It's true that the

---

[1] "Warren Buffett's '2 List' Strategy: How to Maximize Your Focus and Master Your Priorities," on James Clear's official website, accessed September 4, 2017, http://jamesclear.com/buffett-focus.

material is out there, and yes, you *could* scale that steep learning curve and do much of this yourself. But if you run a successful business, or aim to one day, you need to prioritize your highest value activities and focus rabidly on those.

As Gary Vaynerchuk says, *"You have to double-down on your strengths and punt your weaknesses."*[2]

If learning the finer details of publishing is not your strength, punt. Don't let the intermediary goal of learning to write and publish inhibit the end goal of growing your business. Enlist help and get over the hump.

This is where the team at Archangel Ink comes in. We bring our years of self-publishing experience, expertise, and industry connections to write your story, produce high-quality books, and get the finished product into the hands of your potential customers.

---

[2]   WeWork, "Gary Vaynerchuk's Keynote at WeWork Boston— March 2016," Facebook, March 26, 2016, https://www.facebook.com/ WeWork/posts/1276661435679246.

In short, we help entrepreneurs and business professionals reach their audience, share their story, and build their brand through self-publishing. We make the process turnkey, and professionalize the finished product, removing bottlenecks to ensure our clients can put their best foot forward.

# CHAPTER 1

## 20 REASONS YOU SHOULD

## WRITE A BOOK

Authors come in myriad forms and write for many reasons. Bob Burnham's *101 Reasons Why You Must Write A Book: How To Make A Six Figure Income By Writing & Publishing Your Own Book* offers a number of reasons to consider publishing. Here are twenty of the biggest reasons for businesspeople:

1. You will be the expert.

2. You will make more money.

3. You can save on advertising.

4. You demonstrate competence.

5. You quickly build a valuable customer list.

6. Others become more aware and conscious of you.

7. You will edge out the competition because few people are writing books.

8. You will gain instant credibility.

9. You will increase sales.

10. You will separate yourself from the competition.

11. You will compel people to do business with you.

12. You will create valuable information products you can sell.

13. You will have a powerful business card.

14. You will attract more business.

15. You will rev up your magnetism and find YOUR crowd attracted to you more than to your competitors.

16. You will boost your professional image.

17. You will create more value for your prospects and customers.

18. You will gain media attention.

19. You will build your business brand.

20. You will have the best leverage for advertising.[3]

---

[3]    List adapted from Bob Burnham, *101 Reasons Why You Must Write A Book: How To Make A Six Figure Income By Writing & Publishing Your Own Book* (Profits Publishing, 2007), iii–v.

Let's zoom in on a handful of those reasons.

## YOU WILL BE THE EXPERT

An expert is someone who has a comprehensive and authoritative knowledge of or skill in a particular area. Writing a book is one of the most effective ways to prove you have that comprehensive authority and gain the trust of prospective customers.

By authoring a book on a particular topic, you distinguish yourself immediately. Competitors who haven't published fall short in comparison, and you'll become a preferred resource for advice and tips in your area of specialty. Demonstrated and in-demand experts command top dollar and justify premium pricing. They can market more easily and experience less price resistance from their customers. By publishing a quality book, you invite yourself to the experts' club in the eyes of your peers and the public.

## YOU WILL MAKE MORE MONEY

Publishing can generate revenue in two ways. The first is what most people think of when they assess the ROI on a project: royalties on the direct sale of your title. The second is a more lateral approach: utilize your book to increase your overall business revenue.

Traditional publishers offer a meager 5–15% royalty on each unit sold. A title retailing for $20 may net its author $1–$3 per sale, for example.

By self-publishing on your own or with the help of a professional service, you retain significantly more per unit, and thus keep more of the proceeds from your book sales. The same retail price of $20 may net its author $10–$15 per unit sold, or possibly more. That means you might sell 5–15 times fewer units but earn equivalent royalties. These figures demonstrate a significant shift in the profitability equation versus traditional publishing.

Moreover, and especially apropos to business owners, you can leverage your authority to sell products, services, coaching, and information in your niche. Your book is your salesperson and ambassador, working twenty-four hours a day, seven days a week. It promotes your brand and builds rapport with your prospects long after you first write and publish it, and the initial capital investment of production has been made.

## YOU WILL COMPEL PEOPLE TO DO BUSINESS WITH YOU

In marketing, high pressure rarely works. Instead, you need to build rapport and compel customers to work with you in a way that *feels authentic* to them. Your book is an easy way to do this. It is devoid of trickery, mind games, or unsavory tactics. Prospects can read it on their own time and approach you on their terms, rather than feeling as though you're breathing down their necks across the desk.

For some, simply seeing that you've published may be reason enough to work with you. Others will become willing to take the plunge once they read your book and accept you as the thought leader they've been seeking. Either way, publishing makes it clear that you know what you're talking about because, at the very least, you have an entire book's worth of information to offer on the subject. You become the obvious choice over a competitor whose only proof of expertise is an impersonal business card or website.

## YOU WILL EDGE OUT THE COMPETITION BECAUSE FEW PEOPLE ARE WRITING BOOKS

Consider this: how many people do you know personally who have written and published a book? If you're outside of the publishing industry or select circles, the answer is probably: not many. This rarity represents an opportunity to position yourself as preeminent in your niche, to get ahead of the curve and establish yourself as a leader. You may sell the same products or provide the same services as your competitors, but the added value, credibility, and insight into your brand that a book offers to your prospects helps sets you apart.

As time goes on, the arms race may escalate, and at some point, it may be requisite to have a book, just as it is today to have a website. If you're an early adopter, you can enter the arena on your own terms. Wait too long, and the choice may be thrust upon you.

# CHAPTER 2

## THE COST OF INACTION:
## REASONS NOT TO DELAY

Content creation is a powerful marketing strategy. Consider the following statistics:

- 96% of B2B buyers want content with more input from industry thought leaders.

- 75% of marketers are increasing investment in content marketing.

- 70% of B2B marketers plan to create more content in 2017 compared to 2016.

- Leads who are nurtured with targeted content produce a 20% increase in sales opportunities.

Businesses want information from other businesses before they buy from them—and your competitors know it. That's why they're hustling to create the kind of content that will position them as experts in the industry. You may not be able to beat out those competitors in a blog-to-blog showdown or a social media standoff. The tool you do have that they're probably not leveraging, though, is a book.

But it's not like this strategy is a secret. You can bet that if we're telling you about it, someone is telling your competitors. If they move more quickly than you, then they'll earn the expert status you're eyeing. If you want those sales before they get them, it's time to jump on this opportunity.

If you're still not convinced, consider this: The opportunity cost of letting someone else step into the coveted role of the expert is huge. You miss out on that status and all the sales that come with it. Then you miss out on the word-of-mouth marketing from those sales, the new clients that marketing will bring in, the repeat sales, the add-on services, the scalable products (courses and AV content) that come with publishing, the new books, and so on.

So, yes, moving into the publishing arena is an investment, and it comes with a cost. But doing nothing comes with a cost as well. Failure to embark on new ambitions is costly. Allowing your company to sputter along and be lapped by hungrier competitors keen to provide value where you won't? That too is costly.

Self-publishing isn't the only way to harness forward momentum, but it's a good way and a tactic still largely untapped. And if you're reading this, consider it an opportunity extended to you.

# CHAPTER 3

## HOW ARCHANGEL INK HELPS
## YOU TELL YOUR STORY

As this publishing model grows in popularity, business professionals are consistently turning to ghostwriting services to help them write their books. Chances are you've heard of ghostwriting, but chances are almost equally good you've heard a disappointing story or two about it. Something like this:

John decided to publish a book to demonstrate his expertise in his niche, share information with his audience, and build his business. As a business coach and consultant, he knew his company wasn't making as much money or bringing in as many clients as it could, and he wanted to change that. Friends in the industry had spoken highly of ghostwriting services, so he decided to give it a try.

Fueled by enthusiasm, John sat down at his desk and put together an outline of his book. He then took the outline to Fiverr, where a ghostwriter promised to do the work quickly and elegantly. All he'd need to do after would be to find a cover, format the book, and put it out there. John handed the project over and then eagerly awaited the results.

He received the manuscript back from the ghostwriter (behind schedule), and read through it. He was crushed. It was disorganized, poorly written, poorly edited, and in no way representative of his proficiency in his field. What had promised to be a boon to his career would prove downright devastating to his credibility were he to publicly put his name on it.

Not only that, even if he could wrangle the content into usable form, he still had to navigate reams of additional challenges:

- cover design

- digital formatting

- print typesetting

- audiobook production

- publishing platforms

- pricing

- overall marketing strategy

- copywriting

- SEO for keywords and categories

- building an author website

Dejected, John hung his head and returned to business as usual, closing the door on an exciting but overwhelming prospect. Why risk getting burned a second, third, or fourth time on an uncertain strategy with a steep learning curve? Better to stick with lackluster (but at least tried-and-true) tactics with fewer question marks.

Judy experienced a similar disappointment during the formatting of her manuscript. Having already written and edited her book, she hired another firm to format it for digital and print editions. Print edition? No problem. But the digital edition? It just wasn't quite right, and even months later, she still had no file in hand.

After several rounds of attempted troubleshooting, the firm said bluntly, "We're not going to complete this. It's taking too long, our per-hour rate has dropped too low, and it's not worth it for us to do any more work. We're done here."

At Archangel Ink, we get it. You might be sold on the value of a book, and you might even consider enlisting help. But who has the know-how to vet quality help as an outsider to the self-publishing industry? And who has time to play conductor, arranging an orchestra of production specialists?

That's why we've worked hard to perfect our process, so we can guarantee our clients a positive experience and a successful finished product. Our ghostwriting team has developed a custom writing process using an outline alongside recorded interviews, which we transcribe and transform into a manuscript that reads like a book in the client's voice. Section by section, we interview and record, then the client reviews and approves of the content so there are no eleventh-hour surprises.

And after the book is complete, we provide an integrated concierge experience: editing, design, formatting, cover art, audio production, and marketing, all under one roof with a dedicated project coordinator to answer your questions. No tracking down freelancers or wasting time scouring message boards to navigate your way through the industry.

Just trustworthy service and guidance to help you succeed.

# CHAPTER 4

## TOP 10 WAYS TO LEVERAGE
## YOUR BOOK

Writing and publishing your book is just the beginning. With your increased credibility, you can begin leveraging your book as a marketing tool and income generator. Here are ten ways to get you started.

## #1 USE YOUR BOOK AS A DOOR OPENER

Your book can unlock networking and advertising opportunities that would otherwise remain closed to you.

"Before I published my book, *The Financial Planning Puzzle: Fitting Your Pieces Together to Create Financial Freedom*, I was told that a book is one of the best business-building tools that you can have," says Jason Silverberg. "It provides you with 'super credibility' and a leg up on the competition. It's also a great way for people to get to know you, like you, and trust you before they do business with you."

Customers don't select businesses to patronize at random. They typically perform at least some basic research before selecting a diet plan, a new dentist, or an online sales mentor. If you want people to choose you as a result of their research, you need more than an online presence: you need to hit that know-like-trust target, which a book can facilitate.

Consider Jason's results:

> *The Financial Planning Puzzle* has been out for three months, and I've generated enough business during this time to pay for the entire project and then some. I've been able to use the book as a springboard to speaking about my signature workshop, the "5 Steps to Solving Your Financial Planning Puzzle," which takes the concepts in the book and shows how you can apply them to your own life.

## #2 USE YOUR BOOK AS A GIVEAWAY

Your book can be an excellent freebie to initiate a customer sales funnel, a giveaway in exchange for your visitor's email address or contact information. You can also promote a giveaway on social media platforms as a way of directing traffic toward your website.

Using your book this way not only builds your direct marketing email list but also pulls your prospects further into your sales funnel. It gives you an opportunity to build rapport and position yourself as an expert your readers can trust above your competitors. Once you have established that connection, they will be more likely to come to you for advice, products, and services.

## #3 USE YOUR BOOK TO GAIN LEVERAGE IN YOUR LOCAL MARKET

Some business owners struggle to gain leverage in their niche. Consider the case of Mandy Blume, author of *Real Food Recovery: The Busy Mom's Guide to Health &*

*Healing with 92 Gluten Free, Casein Free (GFCF) Recipes.*
Mandy was a bona fide authority, yet her expertise
outpaced her reach:

> When we found tremendous success helping chil-
> dren-at-risk get healthy, I knew that it needed
> to be shared. I started a non-profit, Real Food
> Recovery, and initiated all of the social media
> venues. With a website and blogging about our
> incredible success, I honestly thought that my
> efforts and experience would be noticed and my
> page would grow fast. That was not the case.
> With all of the competition out there—even
> from people whom I knew were not as success-
> ful working with children—the MDs, NDs, DCs
> were growing faster.

Mandy's book was the door opener that finally allowed
her to become a trusted name in her niche and leverage
her market effectively. Since publishing, Mandy
describes: "I have been asked to speak in several venues
dealing with children, food, and cancer. I am able to sell

my book at these events, and the revenue is fantastic. I receive donations from wonderful companies. And accomplishing the 'bucket list' goal of writing a book is one of the best business decisions I have made. It catapulted me into a league that social media did not provide."

Or take the case of Lynda Goldman:

> I had launched a business providing business etiquette presentations but was not getting much business. Then I wrote a book called *How to Make a Million Dollar First Impression.* I was doing a lot of networking, and I went to a sales event, carrying my book with me. Sales reps started coming over to me and literally taking the book out of my hands and giving me $20. I knew I had found my market.

> My newest book, *Write to Heal: 7 Steps to Write and Publish a Wellness Book that Heals More People, Makes You the Authority and Leaves Your Legacy*, is a lead-generation tool to find motivated health

providers who will be part of my mastermind coaching group, and take my course on how to write a wellness book.

# #4 USE YOUR BOOK TO FACILITATE EFFECTIVE COLLABORATION WITH CLIENTS

One of the biggest problems with client work is that you can't always tell immediately if you'll be a good fit for working together. Moreover, clients may not understand how you work, and explaining it to them can be a costly time sink. Instead, you can encourage them to read your book. Whether you're just kicking off your relationship, starting a new project, or clearing up confusion, this is an excellent tool.

Once they're through, you have a clear runway for getting down to business. As an added bonus, you've just cemented the client's perception of your expertise. If they didn't already view you as a credible authority, they do now.

# #5 USE YOUR BOOK TO ENHANCE YOUR CREDIBILITY

Your book offers an opportunity to demonstrate your insight, and that transparency builds trust. Many business owners mistakenly hamstring themselves by refusing to share what they know.

"One of the biggest fears of self-publishing is that people will 'steal' your ideas and expertise," explains Alex Goldstein, author of *Publish To Sell: Long Term Income from Short Term Effort*. "But you should drop the objection that you shouldn't be transparent—people who hire you will gain trust from full disclosure. People who will use your transparency to do it themselves weren't going to hire you anyway."

Mandy Blume's story also demonstrates this. Her book earned her invitations to speak as well as donations, and it propelled her to prominence.

When you mention "my book," people immediately revise their assumptions about you in their minds. All else being equal, a published author carries more credibility than Joe Shmoe "expert," period.

# #6 USE YOUR BOOK TO COMMUNICATE YOUR CORE BUSINESS MISSION

As a business owner, it's easy to go full speed ahead in your business, putting out one fire after the next, bringing on new clients, and dealing with your mounting task list. Because of this, it's common for businesses to function without a core mission to guide them. That's a problem, though, because a business without a mission often lacks the focus and structure necessary for growth.

Sitting down to write a book is an opportunity to reflect on your priorities and clarify your business's core mission. Your theme and mission will reciprocally inform each other. Deliberately crafting your book will help you articulate your vision and identify your ideal customers and how best to serve them.

# #7 USE YOUR BOOK TO INCREASE YOUR ONLINE FOOTPRINT

Your online "footprint" is the totality of your presence on the Internet. Why does your footprint matter? Because it represents what prospects will see when searching for you online, and the strength and reputation of that footprint will influence whether they opt to work with you.

So you need to curate your brand, paying particular attention to the quality of all the social media posts, blog posts, comments and shares, articles, courses and more, in which you're referenced. Anytime you can positively expand this footprint, you should, and that's exactly what your book does. Each share, blog post reference, and book mention gives you another opportunity to engage with your audience in a constructive, meaningful way.

# #8 USE YOUR BOOK TO DEMONSTRATE THOUGHT LEADERSHIP

Thought leaders are influencers whose opinions and ideas set the tone for entire industry discussions. As a thought leader, you will become the go-to expert in your field, a trusted source who can inspire and pave a path of success. This is exactly what happened to Jay Campbell, author of *The Definitive Testosterone Replacement Therapy MANual: How to Optimize Your Testosterone for Lifelong Health and Happiness.*

> With the added authority that being a number one bestselling author affords me, I've launched and expanded a number of health and hormonal optimization-related businesses, including TRT Revolution and Optimized Life Nutrition. I've also partnered with a nationwide medical provider to help make hormone replacement therapy available to millions of Americans.

Jay goes on to say, "The book has performed incredibly, and as of this writing, is the all-time top-rated TRT book on Amazon. In addition to the revenue earned from direct sales in digital, paperback, and audio formats, I also make the book available as a free + shipping offer to those who opt into my site. Because the book is incredible and over-delivers on value, it further builds trust and credibility among my audience, facilitates continual new and high-quality reviews, and provides ancillary income through the steady stream of leads to market our other products and services."

Imagine how your ideas, processes, and innovation can set you apart as a thought leader in your industry.

## #9 USE YOUR BOOK AS A BRIDGE TO OTHER PRODUCTS AND SERVICES

One of the best ways to leverage your book is to think of it not as a finish line, but as a gateway. With a book as an introduction, you can expand the material into a course, as Marco LeRoc has done. Marco explains:

With the launch of my latest book, *Activate Your Untapped Potential*, I realize that authors can build a profitable business around their books [instead of] just selling them.

All of a sudden, you become the expert, the go-to person, and the celebrity. Because of my books, I have been featured on many news outlets locally, nationally, and internationally. What a great way to build my brand!

I am also coaching and developing a course around my books. The best part of all is getting the paid speaking engagements and being able to make an impact on many around the globe.

Digital course content and trainings in particular have the added benefit of scalability. Once they're created, you can escape trading time for money and generate concurrent passive revenue streams.

Your book is just the first step to maximizing your potential offerings to customers and developing additional revenue streams. What doors can your book open for you?

## #10 USE YOUR BOOK TO CONNECT WITH INDUSTRY LEADERS

Connecting with other industry leaders is a crucial way to build your influence, and it can happen on many levels. You can approach others in your field, for instance, to ask them to review your book.

Some will be happy to do so, and now you're on their radar. Offer something in return, and if they accept, chances are good you'll forge a relationship for which your book was an organic pretext.

Your book also offers the potential to kick off a long-term sales or B2B relationship. As Jason Silverberg explains, "I've also gifted the book to some key decision makers to help provide an introduction to me before I call them to schedule a face-to-face meeting. It's been a tremendous door opener."

Keep in mind that an industry leader doesn't have to be a person; it can be a business network as well. Lynda shares her experience after writing her book:

> I started getting calls to give seminars at many large companies, mainly in the pharmaceutical industry, because they give their sales people more training than other industries. But I also gave seminars at technology companies and financial institutions. My book helped me build my seminar business, which later expanded to creating training programs in related areas, such as leadership, sales, and marketing.

Through the publication of this one book, Lynda found a whole niche just waiting to soak up her expertise and call her a leader. What unexpected opportunities await you?

# CHAPTER 5

## TESTIMONIALS

Consider these testimonies of businesspeople who partnered with Archangel Ink to publish their book as a tool to power their business.

While the process was an uphill battle at times, writing and publishing *The Financial Planning Puzzle: Fitting Your Pieces Together to Create Financial Freedom* has elevated my financial planning practice to the next level. Rob and his team at Archangel Ink were instrumental in helping me get my book out quickly and efficiently. If you're on the fence about writing a book and you're serious about growing your business, I would take the time to invest in the next chapter of your business.

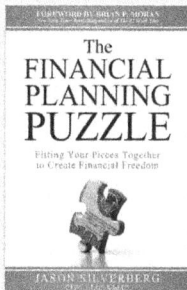

~ Jason Silverberg, author of:

*The Financial Planning Puzzle: Fitting Your Pieces Together to Create Financial Freedom*

With the rock star team at Archangel Ink, I'm now able to secure speaking gigs and have grown my podcast downloads by over 40 percent in only three months since launching my book, *UnResolution: How to Ditch Resolutions Forever, Live Life by Design, and Achieve Your Dreams.*

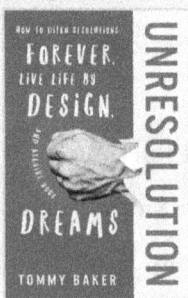

~ Tommy Baker, author of:
*UnResolution: How to Ditch Resolutions Forever, Live Life by Design, and Achieve Your Dreams*

Some publishers were interested [in my book], but as a new name, my "cut" would be $1 from a $25 book. This seemed incredibly low. Then I found Archangel Ink. It is the best of both worlds. They would edit and act as a publisher, but I would pay for that service and completely own all the rights to my book.

There was guidance for the launch and social media advice. My book hit bestseller in the category of "Children's Health" and 8th in "Gluten Free." I am consistently selling books every month. [T]he advice given turned out to be incredibly true. Being an author exudes a different air.

Writing a book was certainly a lot of work, but Archangel Ink made it quite beautiful in the end.

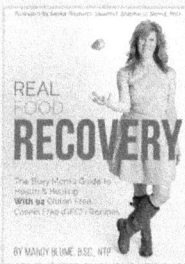

~ Mandy Blume, author of:
*Real Food Recovery: The Busy Mom's Guide to Health & Healing with 92 Gluten Free, Casein Free (GFCF) Recipes*

I spent many months working on *The Definitive Testosterone Replacement Therapy MANual: How to Optimize Your Testosterone for Lifelong Health and Happiness*. As a successful fitness model, coach, and realtor, I know the value of a book as a working business card … I know the process of book writing and publishing can be daunting. But it's been absolutely worth it in my case as a marketing tool, lead generator, and credibility enhancer. I'd estimate that it's led to $100,000 in additional yearly revenue.

On a personal note, Rob and his team have been great to work with. I know he cares about my success, and he's made sure to go the extra mile to do things right and not take shortcuts. They provide premier service for authors looking to stand out and self-publish professionally.

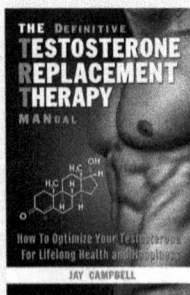

~ Jay Campbell, author of:
*The Definitive Testosterone Replacement Therapy MANual: How to Optimize Your Testosterone for Lifelong Health and Happiness*

# EPILOGUE

If you're like most, you still have hesitations about why self-publishing isn't for you. Despite all the good reasons to do it, it can still be frightening. You're staking a claim to your expertise and competence, and if you fall on your face, everyone will see.

The good news? With the right help, you minimize the downside and maximize your opportunity. The benefits of publishing your own book—or in many cases, books—are simply too numerous to ignore. You will become the expert. You will build rapport with your clients and prospective customers. You will grow your list and move your target audience toward and down the sales funnel. You will clarify your mission and experience an increase in profits and opportunities that you simply wouldn't without your book.

Keep in mind that the first book is only the beginning. Getting started now will open the door to more books and content-creation opportunities. Once your readers see you as a credible authority and thought leader, their trust in you will grow alongside their willingness to enlist you to provide solutions for their problems.

With professional help to streamline the experience, you can write and publish your book now, with minimal stress. And you can take advantage of the medium before your competitors do. Excuses will always be there, but the opportunity won't—which is why it's time to get started right away.

At Archangel Ink, our goal is to help business owners and entrepreneurs just like you publish easy-to-leverage, credibility-boosting work. We want to help you share your story and build your brand. And we'll be right here when it's time to publish the next one. To your success!

# ABOUT THE AUTHOR

Rob Archangel here, logophile, communication enthusiast and self-publisher. Several years ago, I worked as an assistant to the publisher of the longest running permaculture journal in North America and got my first taste of the publishing world. Long passionate about writing and communication, I partnered with Matt Stone in 2012 to expand the reach of his site, www.180degreehealth.com, and spearheaded his entry into the eReader, print-on-demand paperback, and audiobook world. Realizing I have a knack and a passion for the process, and that all my time spent learning the ropes could be of value to others, he and I founded Archangel Ink as an umbrella outfit for all one's independent publishing needs. My goal to help authors and entre-preneurs everywhere easily reach their audience, share their message and build their brand. From cover design and editing, to eBook and paperback formatting, to audiobook production and ghostwriting, Archangel Ink is designed to make the process as simple and turnkey as possible for authors and businesspeople to professionalize their written work and focus their energies on whatever it is they do best.